# Messy Molly

Written by Charnan Simon • Illustrated by Mernie Gallagher-Cole

Published in the United States of America by The Child's World®
PO Box 326 • Chanhassen, MN 55317-0326
800-599-READ • www.childsworld.com

## Reading Adviser

Cecilia Minden-Cupp, PhD, Former Language and Literacy Program Director,
Harvard Graduate School of Education, Cambridge, Massachusetts

## Acknowledgments

The Child's World®: Mary Berendes, Publishing Director

Editorial Directions, Inc.: E. Russell Primm, Editorial Director and Project Manager; Katie Marsico,
Associate Editor; Judith Shiffer, Assistant Editor; Caroline Wood, Editorial Assistant

The Design Lab: Kathleen Petelinsek, Design and Art Production

## Library of Congress Cataloging-in-Publication Data

Simon, Charnan.
  Messy Molly / written by Charnan Simon ; illustrated by Mernie Gallagher-Cole.
    p. cm.  (Magic door to learning)
  Summary: Molly claims to be too busy to tidy up when she makes a mess, but things change
when Grandma invites her for a sleepover and she cannot find her Sloppy Bear.
  ISBN 1-59296-625-X (library bound : alk. paper)
  [1. Orderliness—Fiction. 2. Cleanliness—Fiction. 3. Lost and found possessions—Fiction.]
I. Gallagher-Cole, Mernie, ill. II. Title. III. Series.
  PZ7.S6035Mes 2006
  [E]—dc22                          2006001408

A book is a door, a magic door.
It can take you places
you have never been before.
Ready? Set?
Turn the page.
Open the door.
Now it is time to explore.

Molly Drum was a messy little girl.

"Molly!" said her mother.
"Please pick your clothes
up off the floor!"

"Molly!" said her father.
"Please stack your blocks when
you're finished building!"

"Molly!" said her brother Jack.
"If you're going to play with my toys, at
least put them away when you're done!"

But Molly was too busy to be tidy.

"I'll do it later!" she called
as she hurried out to play.

13

One day, Grandma
came over for lunch.
"Molly," said Grandma
as they ate their soup,
"how would you like
to have a sleepover at
my house tonight?"

"YES!" said Molly.
Sleepovers at Grandma's
house were the best!
Jack went last week.
Now it was Molly's turn.
"I'll get Sloppy Bear and
my toothbrush!"

But Molly couldn't find
Sloppy Bear anywhere.
"Help!" Molly cried.
"Sloppy Bear is lost!
I can't go on a sleepover
without him! I have to
find Sloppy Bear! Help!"

"Molly!" her mother said as the whole family came into Molly's room. "Let's do this right!"

Molly's mother helped fold her clothes. Molly's father helped stack her blocks. Jack helped put away toys. Grandma helped make her bed and clear her desk.

And finally, when the room was nice and tidy—"Sloppy Bear!" cried Molly. "You weren't lost after all!"

Our story is over, but there is still much to explore beyond the magic door!

Did you know that cleaning can actually be fun—and a good way to help other people? Talk to your friends about creating an official Cleaning Day when you go through all the toys in your room. Are there some you don't play with anymore? Set these aside in a box, along with any clothes you've outgrown. Have your friends bring their boxes to your house. Talk to an adult about an organization in your neighborhood that might be able to give these items to kids who don't have as much as you do. Your room will be less messy, and you'll get to help someone in need!

These books will help you explore at the library and at home:
Luciani, Brigitte, Vanessa Hié (illustrator), and J. Alison James (translator).
  *Those Messy Hempels.* New York: North-South Books, 2004.
McKissack, Patricia, Fredrick McKissack, and Dana Regan (illustrator).
  *Messy Bessey's Garden.* Danbury, Conn.: Children's Press, 2002.

## About the Author

Charnan Simon lives in Madison, Wisconsin, where she can usually be found sitting at her desk and writing books, unless she is sitting at her desk and looking out the window. Charnan has one husband, two daughters, and two very helpful cats.

## About the Illustrator

Mernie Gallagher-Cole lives in a messy house in Pennsylvania with her husband Rick, daughter Glenna, and son Ian. She would love to live in a clean house someday.